THE TIBER

THE ROMAN RIVER

NORA NOWLAN

Map by Fred Kliem

GARRARD PUBLISHING COMPANY
CHAMPAIGN, ILLINOIS

THIS BOOK WAS EDITED AND DESIGNED
UNDER THE SUPERVISION OF NANCY LARRICK, ED.D.

For assistance in checking the accuracy of the text,
the author and editor are indebted to Brother Romuald
of the Collegio Internazionale Fratelli Maristi, Rome.
Traveling by train, bus, an antique Fiat, and finally
on foot, Brother Romuald reached the source of the
Tiber to make the photograph on page 14.

The photographs on the endpapers are a woman of
Rome and the St. Angelo Bridge across the Tiber in
Rome. Both are from P.I.P.

Copyright © 1967 by Nora Nowlan

One of the monsters of Bomarzo. See page 46 for more pictures.

Contents

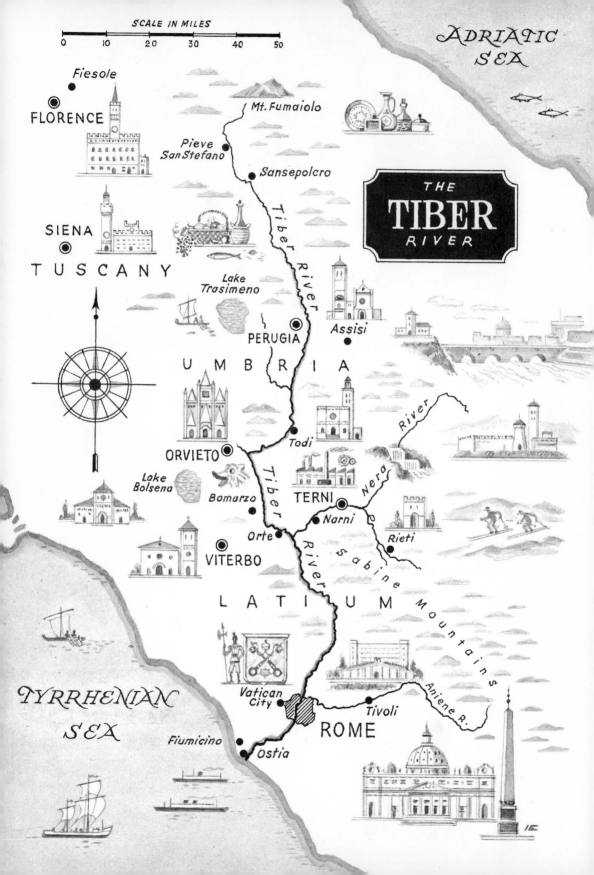

The Roman River

"By Jupiter, Brother! What will you do if the enemy does this?" mocked Remus as he leaped over the wall his brother Romulus was building.

Romulus straightened his back and replied angrily, "I shall do this!" Drawing his sword, he slew Remus. As he wiped the blade he muttered fiercely, "So perish all those who leap over these walls!"

This is said to have happened more than 700 years before Christ was born. Romulus was building the walls of Rome, the city through which the Tiber flows.

Legend says that Romulus and Remus were the twin sons of Mars, the pagan god of war. Their wicked uncle, Amulius, was the reigning king.

Fearing that when the twins grew up they would claim the throne, he decided to get rid of them. He put the infants on a raft and set it adrift on the flooded river.

Father Tiber, the river god, protected them. The raft was washed ashore. A she-wolf found the children and nursed them as though they were her own puppies. When they grew up to be strong men, Romulus began to build his city on one of the seven hills overlooking the Tiber Valley.

The Tiber is not the largest, the most beautiful, nor the most useful river in Italy. Virgil, the Roman poet, described it as the river "having fast eddies and yellow with much mud." Because it is muddy and dull, it is called "the tawny Tiber." Yet this famous river has wound its way through the history of Europe and still winds its way under the 20 bridges of bustling, modern Rome.

The Romans have never forgotten the she-wolf who suckled the famous twins. A wolf and her mate are always kept in a large cage on Capitoline Hill to honor the famous animal.

Italy is a peninsula jutting south into the tide-

The famous she-wolf is sculptured on Rome's new Bridge of Freedom.

less Mediterranean Sea which separates Europe from Africa. On a map Italy looks like a cowboy's high-heeled boot. The Apennine Mountains run down the center from north to south. The Tiber flows through the middle of the country, divides below Rome and enters the sea as twin rivers at

7

Fiumicino and Ostia. Rome is about 20 miles up river.

The first Romans were the people of a little kingdom called Latium, close to the Tiber. They became very powerful and by 276 B.C. were rulers of all Italy. Then they set out to conquer their neighbors. Roman legions marched north, south, east, and west, ever winning new lands. Roman galleys swept the seas, and the eagle symbol of Roman power spread its wings far and wide.

A Roman citizen, or freeman, was an important person. He had the right to wear the toga, or cloak. He could vote and help draft laws. The citizen was entitled to the protection of Rome wherever its flag flew. At one time a man wearing the toga could travel unmolested around the shores of the Mediterranean Sea, east to Persia, through Europe, and across the channel to England.

For 2,000 years Rome was the core of military power, art, and literature in Europe. Its soldiers, scholars, artists, and engineers carried their skills to conquered lands.

The Roman way of life affects the way we live

Rome's most famous road, the Appian Way, 2,000 years ago and today.

in this twentieth century. Our alphabet is Roman, and most books are printed in Roman letters. Because England was conquered by Rome, the English language is rich in words first used by the people of Latium. Italian, Spanish, and French are known as the Romance languages because they all grew out of the tongue spoken by their Roman rulers. The month of March is named for Mars, father of Romulus and Remus. July is named after Julius Caesar and August after Augustus Caesar, both Roman emperors. Lawyers study Roman law, and architects study Roman buildings. Engineers have learned much about road-making, bridge-building, water supplies, and drainage from the work of ancient Romans.

Some years after Christ's crucifixion, Peter, the fisherman of Galilee, went to Rome to preach his Master's gospel of love and peace. It was by the Tiber that he walked, and he may have bathed his dusty, weary feet in its murky waters. The Romans did not want to hear of peace and brotherly love. Peter was seized, imprisoned, and crucified not far from the rushing Tiber. Fiercely, he insisted that he was unworthy to die like his Master, so he was crucified head downward.

Today, nearly 2,000 years after his death, the mighty dome of St. Peter's Church towers over the city of Rome. The church took nearly 200 years to build, from 1450 to 1626. Each year millions of pilgrims come to pray at the fisherman's tomb and to receive the blessing of the Pope.

Armies of ancient Rome returned triumphantly from far lands, trumpets sounding and banners flying. Their prisoners, princes and chieftains, were bound in chains. But the conquerors could not control their wayward river. Each year the rainy season brought floods, and the floods brought death, disease, and famine. Farms were flooded, and food supplies coming to the city by boat were cut off.

The first account of the Tiber floods was written in the fifth century B.C. The problem was a vast one for rulers, engineers, and the common people. Dams and canals were built to control the waters. Centuries later, the problem was solved another way. Just a little over 100 years ago great walls were built which at last chained the angry Tiber.

South of Rome, this family seeks high ground as the Tiber overflows.

Why does the river flood so badly and why does it not sparkle and dance under the high blue sky? The answer to these questions begins 200 miles north of Rome on the eastern side of Mont Fumaiolo, the Chimney Stack Mountain.

12

At the Beginning

In spite of its name, the Chimney Stack Mountain is not a volcano. In winter, wisps of cloud make it look like a smoking chimney. A road runs part way up the mountain to a forest clearing. From this point a path leads upward through the beech woods to a spring only 400 feet below the summit of the 4,584-foot mountain. Water from the spring runs to a marble column bearing the words, "Here rises the river sacred to the destiny of Rome." The eagle of Rome spreads its wings from the top of the column. On three sides are wolves' heads, each holding a bronze ring in its mouth.

The infant river flows in a shallow moat around the column. Then, as a crystal-clear stream about eight inches wide, it starts its twisting journey to

The girl is leaning toward the spring where the Tiber begins.

the sea. It falls 1,000 feet in the first two and one-half miles as it flows through barren land where beech, brooms and briers scrabble for a hold on shallow soil.

On and on the Tiber tears through the valley, still running clear over gravel beds. It is spanned by ancient wooden bridges, which seem absurdly high for such a small stream. When the snow melts in spring, torrents pour from the mountain slopes into the deep valley. The little river swells with icy water as it cascades downhill. When the last snows have melted, the streams dwindle to trickles. The Tiber babbles along cheerfully over stones.

Summer cloudbursts and thunderstorms may send the streams spilling down for an hour or two, but for weeks there may be no rain. Autumn brings terrible thunderstorms and lashing rain. The chattering little stream turns into a swiftly moving brown snake, relentlessly sliding through the valley, sparing nothing. Because the Tiber flows mainly between hills, sudden floods occur along most of its length.

The first town on the river is Pieve San Stefano. In 1944 the town was destroyed by the German army. It was part of their Gothic defense line. All the houses were mined and blown up, and many of the townspeople were killed. The town was rebuilt after the war. Children play around the wide streets, buy *gelati* (ice cream) in bright modern shops and go to a new school.

Sometimes they ask why their town is different from nearby towns. These have thick walls, narrow streets, and old buildings. Old men sunning themselves on the church steps shake their heads and pray that these happy little ones may never know the horrors they remember. The neighboring town of Sansepolcro has a grim memorial to those who died in the war. In a shallow pool below the monument there is a child's skull.

Rising steeply on both sides of the Tiber are great oak forests. The mountain folk say that in the days of wooden ships, trees were floated down to the shipyards on the floods. The wood was made into Roman galleys.

There are quail, pheasants, hares, and partridges on the mountains. Black truffles grow underground. These warty fungi, rather like potatoes, are prized by Italian cooks. They are also prized by pigs, which can smell them out and then root them up with their snouts. Truffle-hunters take pigs out on chains to find them. When the pig starts to root,

The sow has found a truffle, but it will go into the man's basket.

it is hauled off and the man gets the truffles. There is a dog called a truffle dog which can do this job, too.

Along its course, the river gets bigger. Thirty-five miles from its source, it enters the province of Umbria. By this time, red sandstone, limestone, and yellow clay have been washed into its stony bed. The water is dull and even under a brilliant blue sky it has a gray and oily look. The crystal-clear stream has been swallowed up by all the waters which have joined it.

Sometimes the river divides into two or three narrow runnels with gravel banks between them.

On a summer day they are a grand place for children to play with boats, to build dams, and to make harbors for model fleets. Poplar trees grow close to the water. Their roots interlace to form a mat which keeps the flood waters from washing the soil away. Poplar wood is used for fuel and made into pulp for paper. There is no coal in central Italy, and so wood is needed for cooking and heating. All thinnings and prunings are collected and stacked in the farmyards.

Umbria has no seacoast. The Tiber has cut a bed through a wide green valley. On either side, range upon range of hills rise. Some are tall and pointed, others low and rounded. In this farming district, wine and olives are the most important crops for export, but corn, fruit, sheep, and cattle are also raised. Red farmhouses stand some distance from the river—it is safer that way. Men and women work in the fields together, starting at sunrise. At midday the siesta begins, and everyone rests for about three hours. When the sun is lower in the sky, the work goes on again until dusk.

Tall haystacks and two working cows in the upper Tiber valley.

Food and Agriculture Organization, United Nations

In this Umbrian vineyard, the vines are supported on pole trellises.

Grapevines are planted at the foot of willow trees which have been severely pruned, or *pollarded*, like town trees. Long poles are put across the trees and the vines grow along them. This is an old-fashioned way of growing vines. Agricultural experts are teaching the peasant farmers to cut the trees and replace them with concrete posts and wire. Precious food and moisture needed for a good grape crop are used by the trees, which produce nothing. But the farmers are easygoing and hard to change.

Most of the plowing is still done with white cattle yoked to wooden plows, as it was when Rome ruled Europe. The cows do the plowing, pull the carts, and bear calves each year. A cow suckles her calf morning, midday, and evening, and works on the farm all day. The bull calves are killed for veal, but the heifer calves carry on the farm work when they grow up.

Corn and grass are grown between the vines. Grassland is scarce, so the animals graze for only a little time each day. Every farm has big hay-stacks close to the house, and many also have tall pink silage towers. Green grass and corn are packed into these towers. When the silage is pressed down, it becomes brown and solid like plug tobacco. It has a rich smell, and the animals love it.

In spring the grapevines are pruned and the precious wood gathered into faggots. Pruning must be done before growth starts, or the sap, which is the plant's blood, runs away and the plant gets weak. The vines must also be sprayed several

Wine is still made the old-fashioned way in many sections of Italy.

Ripened grapes for wine-making are dumped into tall wooden tubs.

times to prevent disease. In September the grapes
are gathered into barrels and taken to the villages
to be made into wine. The scent of fermenting
grapes hangs in the air. Some wines are never
sent away since they spoil when moved about. But
Orvieto, the Umbrian wine which is known by
everyone who likes to drink good wine, is bottled
in a straw-covered flask called a *fiasco*. This flask
is a familiar sight everywhere in the world.

The best wine is made after a sunny summer,
which is called a "vintage" year. Everyone puts
on his best clothes and goes to church to thank
God for the good harvest. Bands play and there is
singing, dancing, and feasting in the villages to
celebrate a happy end to the year's hard work.

23

The great gate of Augustus Caesar, constructed 2,000 years ago.

A Palace and Pigeons in Perugia

Perugia is the chief city in Umbria. Perched on top of a hill 1,600 feet above sea level, it is interesting, ancient, and beautiful. It is a windy town. In winter an icy wind swirls across from the snow-covered mountains, and in summer the hot wind from Africa called the *sirocco* blows dust through the streets.

Before the Romans came north, Perugia was an

24

Perugia has modern apartments as well as many ancient buildings.

Etruscan city. The Etruscans came from Asia Minor and ruled central Italy for centuries before Christ. To defend their towns, they built walls with huge blocks of stone. Part of these walls and a city gate are still standing.

Etruscans baked the local red clay and made *terra cotta* ornaments. The little town of Deruta, close to the Tiber, is a pottery town. Red clay is used to make crockery, some of modern design, but much is copied from the old Etruscan ware.

The city of Perugia was rebuilt by Augustus Caesar. Even today, one entrance to the city is called the Gate of Augustus.

The Palazzo (Palace) dei Priori is much newer.

This Perugian griffon may be 2,700 years old.

It is only 700 years old. The sandstone steps are worn by many feet, and sconces for holding torches are still on the walls.

On either side of the grand doorway is a statue of the Perugian griffon. This is a mythical animal with a lion's body and an eagle's head and claws. These two griffons are holding down calves with their claws. The butchers of the town gave a lot of money toward building the palace, so the city fathers included the calf in the decoration of the doorway.

Near the steps of the cathedral a fountain plays. The water flows from the mouths of lions, horses, goats, and strange unknown beasts. Each day, as the cathedral clock sounds the first stroke of twelve, there is a whirring in the air as the pigeons of Perugia alight on the steps. Promptly on the last stroke, the great door opens and a man scatters golden corn on the steps. When the birds have

Feeding the pigeons is a tradition among the people of Perugia.

fed, they fly in twos and threes to drink daintily from the spouts of water. Ten minutes later there is not one to be seen. They are preening themselves on the rooftops.

Years ago, important bishops sometimes preached from the open-air pulpit outside the cathedral. Lepers then gathered to hear a sermon or to pick up the alms flung to them. They lived in camps outside the town and were not allowed to mix with other people.

Italian churches are open every day. They are cool, dark, richly decorated, and never empty. Tourists and students stand in groups. Old people sit quietly beside weary mothers who slip in to rest and say a prayer on their way home from shopping. Children come to church to learn prayers and hymns, and of course they scuffle and giggle as children do everywhere.

Perugia is a university town, and the streets are full of chattering students. Many come from all over the world to study Italian history, literature, and art. All Italian students of agriculture must come to Perugia to study for a degree.

Small European cars whiz through the Piazza Garibaldi in Perugia.

Italians know how to hasten slowly. Business is brisk in Perugia and traffic is terrifying. Yet groups of businessmen talk and laugh as they sip wine or little cups of black coffee. "Why hurry?" they say. "Today is ours, and we have wine and the sun. God is good. Why worry about tomorrow?"

Like all Italians, the Perugians are gay and friendly. They expect others to be as gracious as they are. A storekeeper will leave his shop to show a smiling visitor to a bus stop. Thanked, he will reply with a flashing smile, a shrug, and the one word *"Prego,"* which means, "You're welcome." A

29

rude person will be ignored, even if he is rich.

Perugia is an up-to-date town. The shops are full of the silks, laces, wines, shoes and leather goods for which Italy is famous. Perugians say their chocolate is the best in Italy. At Easter the shops have thousands of decorated Easter eggs. Some have designs of colored sugar. Some are hand-painted, and even the littlest one has a surprise hidden in it. A big chocolate egg for a lady may hold expensive perfume. A little girl may find a sparkling ring or a china mouse in hers. People shop in the *supermercato* as well as in the friendly family shops.

Irishmen like potatoes, Frenchmen like bread, Chinese like rice, and Italians like *pasta*. Pasta, which is made from flour, water, eggs, and sometimes olive oil, includes all kinds of macaroni and spaghetti. It is also cut into fancy shapes which have lovely names like *farfalle* (butterflies), *conchiglia* (seashells), and *per i baci* (kiss-bringers). Pasta is eaten in every house at least once a day. It used to be made at home, but now most people buy it. The pasta is served with sauces, and with meat, fish, cheese or tomatoes—plus oil and garlic.

From the Etruscan gate of Perugia, there is a wonderful view of the city. Rusty red roofs spread away to the hills. Houses are mostly roofed with pantiles, which are overlapping tiles made of baked clay, originally used by the Romans. Many roofs have strange, crooked chimney pots sprouting out of them, like the chimneys of a goblin town.

The Umbrian hills turn damson-purple as the orange sun sinks behind them. A melon-slice moon hangs in the velvety sky. People hurry home as the stars begin to twinkle, and the lights of this magic city are flung far and wide like jeweled necklaces.

When it reaches Perugia, the Tiber has grown from stream to river.
Kevin I. Nowlan

The Little Poor Man

The Valley of the Saints lies between Perugia and Assisi. Three of Christ's greatest servants lived and worked here: St. Benedict, St. Clare, and St. Francis of Assisi.

Assisi is built on a hill, and a white winding road leads up to it. On the hillside, dark Italian cypresses stand erect like slender nuns or cluster together as neighbors do outside a church. It is not a very big town, but 800 years ago one of the world's best loved men was born there. History called him St. Francis of Assisi, and the Italians fondly speak of him as *Il Poverello*—The Little Poor Man.

Francis' father was a rich cloth merchant. He journeyed to far countries and brought back gor-

geous fabrics, which he sold to the noblemen of
Assisi. Francis grew up in a wealthy, happy home.
He was gay and had lots of friends. He loved
music and poetry and had a sweet voice. Late into
the warm nights, the walls of the old town echoed
with the songs and laughter of Francis and his
friends. The old people used to wag their fingers
and say, "No good will come of this. He is too
fond of gaiety and fine clothes. He spends too
much money."

His mother was wise, for she knew her son. She
knew that however thoughtless and wild he seemed,
he was always kind and generous to people in
trouble. "Don't worry," she would say to her
husband. "You'll see. One day he will belong
to God."

The Perugians and the Assisians were often at
war with each other. Francis was captured, and
for a year he and his friends were prisoners.
Francis never lost heart but cheered up his friends
and was always especially nice to the prisoners
who had no friends.

Free again, Francis took up his gay life. At

The church built in honor of St. Francis towers over hilly Assisi.

twenty-five, he became ill with fever. When he recovered, he had changed. Everything was different. Now he no longer cared for parties and fine clothes. He felt that he was wasting his life.

Francis had always had a horror of getting leprosy. This disease rotted a man away and forced him to live as an outcast from friends and family.

34

Lepers had to carry a bell to warn people that they were about and call out the dreadful words, "Unclean, unclean." A strange thing happened one day when Francis met a leper. He leaped from his horse, put his arms around the leper, and gave him his cloak and all his money.

Francis then left his father's house and said goodbye to his gay friends. Barefooted and dressed only in a peasant's coarse garment, he went out to the lepers' camp. He lived with them—nursing, comforting, and begging food and clothes for them.

Everyone said he had gone mad. But Francis wasn't a bit mad. He had learned what all little children and wise men know. Loving and being loved is the secret of true happiness. Money can buy power, grand clothes, and fine companions, but it cannot buy love. Francis loved the kiss of the sun, the tug of the wind at his hair, the bite of the frost, and the rain-drenched earth. The silver moon, the golden sun, dancing flames, singing birds, even the insects reminded him of God's goodness in making a beautiful world.

He had a strange power over all living creatures.

The birds and beasts seemed to know he was different from other people. As he walked, birds lit on his shoulders and arms, singing sweetly. When he moved, they flew in a great cloud around his head. When he spoke, they kept quite silent until he had finished. A wolf that was the terror of Assisi followed him around like a dog.

Francis spoke always of God's love for all His creatures, rich or poor, clever or stupid, good or bad, whatever their religion or their color.

Others joined Francis and they too gave up everything they owned. Dressed like poor shepherds, they slept in barns, working each day for their food but taking no money. Everywhere they went they preached of brotherly love, and they sang because they were happy. Everyone who looked into Francis' kind eyes and heard him tell of God's love felt braver and happier.

Francis went to Rome to ask the Pope to give his blessing to their work. At this time, only people of noble families were well educated. The Popes came from these families and lived in magnificent palaces. Some of them had forgotten

St. Francis made friends with birds, sheep, and even a fierce wolf.

that Christ was a carpenter and that Peter, the first Pope, was a poor fisherman. The Pope did not want to see this man who was dressed in peasant's clothes. He thought it was undignified for Francis to go around like a beggar, preaching humility and love of all creatures. Francis was sent away.

Soon after, the Pope had a terrifying dream in which he saw his church toppling over and Francis holding it up. He sent for The Little Poor Man and gave permission for him to go about his work.

Ever since then the followers of St. Francis have been preaching, teaching, nursing, comforting, and helping people all over the world. The army of The Little Poor Brothers in their brown-cowled habits, white girdles, and sandaled feet, grew and grew. By the eighteenth century there were 150,000.

It was a Franciscan friar who stood beside Christopher Columbus when he landed in the New World. Together they knelt and thanked God for their safe journey. A Franciscan built a church in honor of The Little Poor Man in the village that was to grow into the city of San Francisco.

On October 4, 1965, Pope Paul VI stood before the United Nations Assembly and pleaded for peace and understanding between men of good will. It was not by accident that he chose this day. It was the feast day of Francis, the man beloved of all men of good will, whatever their faith. The Little Poor Man spoke for all honest men when he prayed, "Lord, make us instruments of Thy peace; where there is hatred, let us sow love; where there is despair, hope; where there is sadness, joy—for Thy truth's sake."

Many Italians buy their greens at vegetable stands in the streets.

P.I.P. Photo

And So to Rome

Grown wider now, the Tiber runs swiftly and falls rapidly as it winds its way below the hilltop town of Todi.

Three ancient walls encircle Todi. The main street is so steep that it rises at the rate of one foot in every five. Quite a climb! Narrow alleys lead off the main street. They look sinister and mysterious, but there are delicious smells of cooking from expensive restaurants. The names on private houses are those of noblemen, lawyers and doctors. Although the houses look forbidding outside, they are lovely inside. Many are built around a courtyard in the Roman style.

Cars whiz up and down the narrow streets. Buses appear in the most unexpected places. All

Todi is perched high on a hill above the Tiber (marked by arrow).

the buses have a peculiar horn of their own, and when they sound, pedestrians flatten themselves against the walls. Air brakes hiss as the buses round sharp corners, but the passengers laugh even when the driver must back up a little to attempt a corner again.

There were three main reasons why such towns were built high above the plain. First, the towns-people were safe from floods and protected against enemies. Second, a cool breeze blew in the summer.

Saints and grapevines are carved in the door of the Todi cathedral.

Third, the lowlands were believed to be unhealthy. People used to think that fever was caused by breathing the bad air that arose from the swamps. The fever was called *malaria*, which means "bad air." Actually, malaria is caused by the bites of certain mosquitoes.

Gnarled olive trees grow on the sheltered hillsides above the river. Olive oil has always been an important food in Italy, and much of the oil is exported. The olive was so important to the Italians it became a symbol of peace and victory. Victors in contests were crowned with a wreath of olive leaves, just as they are today in the Olympic Games.

The olive is an evergreen tree. It has an oval fruit which is greenish-yellow; some varieties turn black when quite ripe. The olives ripen in October and are gathered in winter and spring. Women put the fruit into baskets and it is taken to the presses. The mixture of pressed oil and juice is left to settle so that grit, twigs, and leaves may sink to the bottom. The oil floats on top of the watery juice and is drawn off.

Oil from the first pressing is the finest and is rarely sold in shops. Some is kept by the grower for his family and friends, and the rest is mixed with the second and third pressings. More than 20 pounds of olives are needed to make a quart of oil. The second and third pressings must be made quickly before the oil becomes rancid. Pits broken in the pressing give the oil a bitter taste.

Just below the town of Todi the river flows through a newly made lake called the Lago di Corbara. It fills a deep gorge and is so new that some of the people near Todi have not heard of it.

Along the river, freshly washed clothes are spread out in the sun. Farmers' wives don't have washing machines so they have a big washday called the *bucato* once a month. Ashes are saved from the wood fires, and a layer of ashes is put into a big wooden tub. The tub is filled up with alternate layers of clothes and ashes with a final layer of ashes on top. Then the tub is filled with cold water and left overnight. Next morning the clothes are washed in the river on a flat stone and spread out to dry in the sun. No patent washing powder ever made clothes so dazzlingly white.

South of Todi and a little west of the river is Bomarzo. This is a large wooded place with great outcroppings of rock which have been carved into strange shapes. They have been there for more

Food and Agriculture Organization, United Nations

One man provides the power for this oldtime olive mill in Umbria.

The monsters of Bomarzo are the stuff that nightmares are made of.

than 500 years. The owner of the place was a soldier and also a student. Bored with the fashionable formal gardens of his rich friends, he planned the "Sacred Wood," as it was called. The place was neglected for years, and trees and bushes grew up around the queer statues. A walk in the wood is full of surprises. You may find yourself

46

Fortunately, the animal on the right is unable to close its jaws.

standing at the feet of a huge elephant, a winged dragon, or a woman who is half-serpent.

At Orte, farther south, the Tiber is joined by the big sparkling river Nera, its most important tributary. The Tiber is now a broad river flowing fast through a wide valley. Its bed is straight and varies from one hundred to one thousand yards wide and is three yards deep at its shallowest part. This stretch of the river is called the Fiasco because it widens to the shape of a flask. It flows about three times faster after the Nera joins it. The rocky land near the Nera is porous. The flood waters drain away into porous rocks and gradually seep back into the river.

South of Orte the river never falls very low in summer. In winter there are terrible floods above Rome, and the entire valley turns into a swirling yellow lake.

Close now to the northern outskirts of Rome, the river flows through farmland. Black and white Friesian cattle and flocks of sheep graze on swampy pastures which have deep drains cut in them. There are brickworks and gravel dredgers by the stony banks.

The hills of Rome sweep down to the valley, and Father Tiber flows into his city under the ancient Ponte Milvio and past the modern Olympic Stadium.

The City of Power

The early Roman kings had to fight hard to keep their kingdoms. One, Tarquin, offended his subjects and was driven out of Rome. He went to a neighboring chief, Lars Porsena, for help. Together they led an army to the walled city which stood on one bank of the Tiber.

Tarquin's troops reached the river and were about to swarm across a narrow bridge. But a brave Roman named Horatius ran across the bridge and with two companions held the invaders back. Behind Horatius, the Romans hacked down the wooden bridge. At the last moment, Horatius ordered his companions to run for their lives. As the bridge collapsed, he plunged into the river and swam under a rain of arrows and spears.

Thomas Macaulay wrote a famous poem about the legend of Horatius. The poet imagined the warrior saying:

> *"O Tiber! Father Tiber!*
> *To whom the Romans pray,*
> *A Roman's life, a Roman's arms,*
> *Take thou in charge this day."*

> *So spake he, and speaking sheathed*
> *The good sword by his side,*
> *And with his harness on his back*
> *Plunged headlong in the tide.*

Horatius reached the bank safely and was well rewarded by his fellow citizens:

> *They gave him of the corn land*
> *That was of the public right.*
> *As much as two strong oxen*
> *Could plow from morn till night.*

The ancient Romans were pagans who worshiped gods of nature and offered sacrifices to them. Jupiter was the father of the gods; Juno was his wife. Venus was the goddess of beauty and Apollo

Authenticated News International

Roman aqueducts, shown in this painting, were engineering marvels.

the sun god. There were many others, each with its own temples. The Romans prayed and offered sacrifices before making any important decision. They believed in omens and judged whether the gods were pleased or angry by the weather, the position of the stars, and the waxing and waning of the moon.

The rich lived in great luxury, but the poor kept alive as best they could. Among the educated classes were skilled engineers and builders. They built magnificent temples to please their gods and grand palaces to live in. There were strong walls around their cities and many straight, paved roads.

As the Romans conquered other countries, they brought back prisoners who were sculptors, artists, silversmiths, and weavers.

Water for Rome came from wells and springs until 312 B.C. when the first aqueduct was dug. In A.D. 144 the great Aqua Marcia was built to carry stream water from the Sabine hills, 44 miles from the city. Remains of the great stone arches on the nearby plain may still be seen. Many of the old Roman houses had piped water from leaden water mains in the streets. Well-to-do families also had central heating.

The rich were vain and took great care of their bodies. The luxurious public baths were like clubs. Here the politicians, lawyers, and rich men went to relax, discuss business, gossip, and gamble. They soaked in warm water and were served food and wine on floating trays. Slaves massaged them with perfumed oils and then, dressed once again in their togas, they went about the business of the city.

The poor people had no share in such luxury, although public baths were supplied for the commoners. Many men and their families were slaves.

The early rulers of Rome were shrewd. They built arenas where they staged magnificent entertainments to please the common people. The largest and most famous was the Colosseum, built more than 1,900 years ago. Its ruins are a landmark in modern Rome.

The Colosseum was circular, with four tiers of stone and marble seats which held 80,000 spectators. The arena could be flooded for mock sea battles. Underneath was a labyrinth of tunnels where wild animals and prisoners were kept. Lions, bears, crocodiles, and elephants were captured in Africa or elsewhere and brought up the Tiber to the city. Trained gladiators fought them with spears and nets. The gladiators also fought one another. If a man had fought well and the crowd liked him, the spectators held their thumbs up as a signal to spare his life. Thumbs down was a vote for death. The final decision was made by the emperor.

Slaves and prisoners were sometimes driven into

The Colosseum when gladiators fought wild beasts, and its ruins.

the arena to fight the beasts. Weak from hunger, they were quickly finished off by the animals. The early Christians, who refused to worship the Roman gods, were also thrown to the lions. But the Christians were not good entertainment. Believing that they would reach Paradise after dying for their religion, they simply prayed while waiting for death. Their quiet bravery amazed the Romans, and many became interested in the new religion.

Chariot racing was a popular sport with the rich young men. They trained on the swampy ground close to the Tiber and were the idols of the ladies. They raced their chariots round and round the arenas. Chariots often overturned when the horses collided, and the drivers were badly injured or killed. Huge bets were made on the races, as on horse races today.

Rome was ruled by strong and cruel men, but gradually the leaders became soft from easy living. The last great emperor, Constantine, moved the capital to the new city of Constantinople (now Istanbul), and adopted Christianity. Northern barbarians invaded Rome. Marble was stripped from palaces and weeds grew in the temples of the gods.

For about 600 years the Tiber rushed through a neglected city occupied by uncivilized peoples. In the sixteenth century, things changed. Trade improved and money poured into Italy. There was a new interest in art and literature. This period was called the Renaissance, or rebirth, of European civilization.

Italy was then divided into many small kingdoms which were continually at war with each other. Little by little, the Catholic Church gained control of much of Italy. Some of the Popes became too interested in the pleasures and treasures of the world. They engaged famous architects to design palaces and splendid churches, and spent fabulous sums on their decoration. Although these Popes betrayed their spiritual trust, they did gather together magnificent treasures and kept them safe.

Wealthy people vied with each other in providing fabulous entertainments. One banker used to give banquets outside his palace overlooking the Tiber. After each course, the silver dishes and plates were thrown into the river. The guests were much

An electric train passes the ruins of an early Roman aqueduct.

impressed by this magnificence. After they had gone home, the servants would haul up the underwater net which had caught the dishes.

57

Carriages like this one before City Hall are still popular in Rome.

Carrozze and Cats

The largest air and rail terminal in the world is the Roman Termini. It is a crossroads for travelers from every continent. In its lofty halls, shops, and restaurants, there is a babble of voices in many languages.

58

As you leave the building and catch your first glimpse of the city, a homely smell makes you sniff and sniff again. Horses! It can't be—not in modern Rome! Then you see the *carrozze* lined up, the horses dozing in the sun or eating out of their nose bags.

The drivers snooze in the back seats of the carriages, play cards, or chat with their friends while they wait for a fare. In summer the horses wear straw hats with flowers in them. Visitors love to ride in a carrozza, and Roman families go shopping in them. Parents, children, fruit, vegetables, and groceries all pile in. At night the clip-clop of horses' feet beats out an accompaniment to velvety voices singing pop songs. Long-haired young Romans like to hitch a ride home with a friendly driver.

Roman traffic seems crazy. Drivers shout abuse at each other and wave their hands in the air. They fume, fret, blow their horns, and argue with the policemen. Still they are always polite to pedestrians. If a pretty girl or an elderly person steps off the pavement, there is a screech of brakes and the traffic stops dead. People step nimbly when they must, but then they stroll along again. Young men ride Vespa scooters, and dark-eyed girls perch sidesaddle on the pillion.

The Fiat is the Italian family car. Models of every size, type and color, even three-wheelers, whiz about.

Sometimes a taxi driver tears through the city with his finger on the horn, crashing the lights. Policemen wave him on, and the traffic parts as if by magic to let him through. Strangers stand and stare, but a Roman will explain: "He carries the Bambino to one who is very ill."

In the Franciscan church on Capitoline Hill, there is a pink-cheeked wooden statue of the Child Jesus. No one is sure where it came from, but it is believed to have power to cure the sick and comfort the dying. It is dressed with jewels from top to toe and is on view in the church. Some years ago a thief stole the gems from the wooden figure. Within a very short time, the Bambino was covered again with jewels and golden ornaments, given by the Roman women.

A traffic policeman in Rome lives longer if he does not get jumpy.

Before the days of automobiles, a prince kept a gilt carriage ready day and night to carry the Bambino to the homes of the sick. Now a taximan carrying the precious passenger gets the right of way through the city's dense traffic.

Each year the Bambino is put in the Christmas crib. On the feast of the coming of the Wise Men, little Roman children, dressed in their best, climb the steps to the church. They stand before the crib and say poems and make speeches. This is the kind of happy gathering that Italians love.

Sick people believe that the bejeweled Bambino will make them well.

Sycamore trees line the sidewalks of Rome, and apricot-colored houses are outlined against the blue sky. There is a surprise around every corner. Ruined temples and palaces are surrounded by modern offices and houses. In the overgrown ruins, scores of half-wild cats slink between broken pillars and sun themselves on crumbling walls. Families and families of cats have lived like this for many generations.

Shopkeepers throw them meat and old ladies bring them milk, but they belong to no one and live chiefly on rats and mice. Since there are few rats in Rome, folk living near these "catteries" are careful to close their windows. The cats are clever thieves and sometimes a dirty, battle-scarred tom will decide to sleep in a comfortable bed.

Exactly 20 cats, or parts of cats, gathered at the Forum of Trajan.

Authenticated News International

In Rome, the Tiber winds between stout walls far below street level. Women with baskets on their heads stroll across the bridges beside sightseers and students. Men sit on the broad paths beside the river, sunbathing or fishing in groups. They lower a large net fixed to a frame into the water. Every now and again they will haul it up to see if they have caught anything. Solitary fishermen use a rod and line. When the river is in flood, the paths are covered and the waters roar through the city.

There is only one island in the Tiber where it flows through Rome. The Isola Tiberina is shaped like a ship and is reached by a bridge, first built 62 years before Christ was born. The Brothers of St. John of God have a hospital on the island, which has been a place of healing since Rome was struck by a pestilence nearly 2,300 years ago. The rulers of the city sent doctors to Greece to consult the physicians at the temple of Aesculapius, the Greek god of healing.

The Greek doctors used snakes in their temples. One of the snakes coiled itself up in the Roman

Kevin I. Nowlan

The bridge to Isola Tiberina was built more than 2,000 years ago.

The sign of Aesculapius on Isola Tiberina, and the modern symbol.

Kevin I. Nowlan

ship and was carried to the Tiber. It slipped overboard and swam to the island. This was taken as a sign that Aesculapius wished a temple to be built there. A temple was built. The place became famous for its cures, and people came from far away to consult the doctors. The sign of Aesculapius— a staff and a serpent—is still clearly visible on the rocky island. This is also the badge of modern doctors of medicine.

Augustus Caesar boasted that he found Rome a city of brick but left it a city of marble. Over the centuries the buildings have been stripped of their marble facings. Even the Colosseum reveals its brickwork where the outer shell of travertine limestone has been destroyed. One dazzling marble monument shines in the sun. It is the immense Victor Emmanuel monument, completed in 1911 after 25 years of labor. A flame burns before the tomb of Italy's Unknown Warrior, taken from a battlefield of World War I. An armed guard stands watch, night and day, alongside the tomb.

Italian policemen are called *carabinieri*. They are magnificent in red and blue uniforms with flowing

Like people everywhere, Romans look out windows.

Toss a coin into the Fountain of Trevi, and you will return to Rome.

cloaks and cocked hats. They wear spotless white gloves and carry swords. Italians love grand clothes, and many uniforms are adapted from the gorgeous raiment of past days.

Rome is famous for its many fountains. Some splash in broad streets and piazzas; others tinkle and murmur in courtyards and narrow streets. Best known to visitors is the Trevi fountain. It is one of the very big ones. A group of figures is carved from volcanic rock. Hidden waterworks send more than 20 jets gushing from the rock into a pool.

There is a belief that anyone who throws a coin into the Trevi fountain will return to Rome before he dies. Everyone wants to go back to Rome, so countless coins from far-off places splash into the water every day. Small boys haunt the place in the hope of fishing out some money, but they rarely get a chance. Each week the pool is cleaned out and the money given to the poor.

Sidewalk cafes are enjoyed by tourists and by the people of Rome.
Italian State Tourist Office

The City of Peace

The great dome of St. Peter's Church towers over the rooftops of Rome. The copper ball and cross 435 feet above the ground are reflected in the Tiber. St. Peter's is the heart of Vatican City and is one of the most magnificent Christian churches in the world.

When Italy became a single kingdom under King Victor Emmanuel, the Popes retired from public life and lived in seclusion at the Vatican. In 1929, by agreement between the State and the Church, the Pope became ruler of Vatican City. It is the smallest state in the world, with only 100 acres and 1,000 inhabitants.

Close to the bridge of St. Angelo, a street leads to the great piazza of St. Peter's. A broad white

Italian State Tourist Office
St. Peter's Church, with the great piazza and obelisk at top right.

line marks the entrance to the Vatican state. There is no barrier, no gate, and no sentry. One step and you are in one of the world's most powerful states.

There is no army. The Pope is protected by 120 Swiss guards. They come from four districts in Switzerland, have had military training, and must be 5′ 11″ tall. They are dressed in brilliant uniforms of red, yellow, and blue and carry eight-foot halberds. They attend the Pope on all his public appearances and stand motionless for hours at a time.

The Vatican museums, art galleries, and libraries are world-famous. The buildings are full of works of art gathered together over hundreds of years. Each day streams of sightseers walk through them, and students pore over priceless documents.

The Pope lives simply in apartments which were once the servants' rooms when the princely Popes succeeded the fisherman Peter. He has an army of advisers who help him in the immense work of governing his world-wide flock. Cardinals, monsignori, and prelates, all experts in some subject, are his assistants. Each day he receives important statesmen and learned men privately, but once a week he is carried in state into the huge church to meet, greet, and bless the thousands of people who flock to St. Peter's.

Two hours before the Pope arrives in the church, crowds gather in the huge piazza, on the broad steps, and by the sparkling fountains. Bearded Greek priests, monks and friars in brown, black,

Two of the Vatican's famous Swiss guards, with 8-foot halberds.

and white robes, and nuns in blue, brown, black, and white habits with many strange headdresses, chat and laugh together. Visitors stand about, carrying cameras. Vendors hawk post cards and souvenirs, and the carrozza drivers do brisk business.

Gradually, the crowd drifts into the immense,

The Pope goes out on a rainy day, escorted by carabinieri.

dim church. Tickets for the audience are free, but the more important visitors get the places with the best view. The church is so beautifully designed that it is difficult to realize how huge it is. Looking high up at a mosaic of St. Mark, you suddenly notice that the pen in his hand is over five feet long. The canopy over the high altar is supported by four columns 95 feet high. They are gilt bronze pillars as twisty and shiny as sugar barley.

The murmur of voices in the church swells to a roar as the Pope, seated in his ceremonial chair, is carried through the great bronze doors. There is a flurry of scarlet- and purple-robed prelates about the foot of the altar as the Holy Father, smiling and spreading his arms in welcome, is carried forward. As he seats himself, a monsignor places a red velvet footstool under his feet. He speaks in turn to people of many nations, using their language so all may understand his message of peace and hope and love. He greets visitors from far away and is answered by cries of, "Viva il Papa!"

Gray-haired women, bent old men, sturdy footballers, ebony-skinned Negroes, almond-eyed orientals, and people of all other races are welcomed.

The Pope comes down the steps to speak to the wide-eyed schoolchildren, who cheer and clap as he walks by. Many gifts are presented, such as beautiful embroidery, paintings, carvings, vestments, gold and silver. These will be sent to needy churches. At Easter time, a sleeping lamb is sometimes laid at his feet. The magnificence of the church and the brilliance of the uniforms are a strange contrast to the figure in plain white cassock, white skull cap, and red velvet slippers.

When the Pope has finished speaking, the crowds move out into the sunlight. Some linger to murmur a prayer at the Michaelangelo "Pieta." This statue of the dead Christ in His mother's arms is one of the most beautiful works of man. It took two years of Michaelangelo's young life to finish it, and the girdle of Mary's image bears his name. It was the only piece of sculpture he ever signed. He was just 24 years old. He was 90 when he died.

In 1964, Pope John agreed to lend the Pieta to the Vatican pavilion at the World's Fair in New York. He said that it should be seen by the many people who could never go to Rome. It was shipped to America, insured for almost $3,000,000. But the Italians wailed, "If anything should happen to it, what good is all that money? There can never be another Pieta." But all went well, and the statue is now safely back in St. Peter's.

Between the fountains in the piazza, there is a stone column 135 feet high. This obelisk was

Michaelangelo's "Pieta" traveled from St. Peter's to New York City.

brought from Greece to decorate pagan Rome nearly 2,000 years ago. In the sixteenth century it was moved in front of St. Peter's. For this mighty task, 900 men, 150 horses, and 47 cranes

77

were used. Crowds gathered to watch and shout advice. They were so noisy that the engineers' orders couldn't be heard.

The Pope was sent for. He ordered absolute silence under pain of death. Then a sailor in the crowd noticed that the ropes were giving under the strain. "Wet the ropes!" he shouted. He was hustled away but not before the engineers had heard and acted on his advice. The ropes held, the pillar was put in place, and, of course, the sailor was forgiven and rewarded.

An overhead passage leads from the Vatican down to the castle of St. Angelo, which was once a prison. Many wretches were dragged through the passage to its dungeons. When the Popes ruled Italy, they often found themselves in great danger. Wrapped in dark cloaks, they too, hurried down the corridor, clambered into a barge, and stole away to safety. The passage fell into disrepair, but recently it has been restored. When asked why, Pope John is said to have replied with a twinkle in his eye, "You never know—it may be needed again."

The castle of St. Angelo, with the Pope's overhead passage at left.

As the sun goes down, the bells of St. Peter's peel out and the red light of Radio Vatican winks in the darkening sky. The powerful station broadcasts in many languages, keeping in touch with the cardinals and bishops far away. During World War II its signal, the bells of St. Peter's, and the calm voice announcing, "This is Radio Vatican," brought hope and comfort to the victims of Hitler and Mussolini.

Fountains and Marshes

Rome is unbearably hot in summer, but the encircling hills are cool. Years ago rich people built summer houses in the hill villages. The villages grew into towns. Tivoli, which is 20 miles northeast of Rome, is one of them. It is only 700 feet above sea level, but it is a paradise compared with the sweltering city. Villas surrounded by olive groves and orchards cover the slopes of the hills.

The town is built on the Aniene River, a large tributary of the Tiber. Aqueducts carried its water to ancient Rome, and their massive ruined arches still stand boldly against the skyline. Hydroelectric plants along the river supply much of the city's electricity.

Near the town there are hot sulphur springs. The

Terraces and tunnels at Villa d'Este.

One of the scores of fountains in the gardens of Villa d'Este.

water bubbles up at 75° Fahrenheit and is bright blue. It smells strongly of rotten eggs, from hydrogen sulphide. This water is said to cure throat, skin, and other ailments. Many Romans go to the Bagni di Tivoli for treatment.

The most famous place in Tivoli is the Villa d'Este. Its fountains and water gardens were built for the pleasure of the owners in the grand Renaissance days. One walk has 100 fountains. The sparkling waters of the Aniene River cascade down terraces, spraying plumes into the air among the tall cypresses.

Artists and engineers devised strange ways of using the water to entertain their wealthy employers. There was an organ worked by water, and the Fountain of the Owl made a noise like an owl's cry. Pranks were played on guests who had to pretend to be amused when their gorgeous clothes were soaked as they stooped to smell a flower. At the Grand Cascade the water leaps over 100 yards as it rushes out of a tunnel, and the spray shows all the colors of the rainbow.

From the hills of Rome, there is a final view of the murky Tiber, flowing toward the Tyrrhenian Sea. The river's last miles are through the Campagna, a flat area known in ancient times as Latium. Here the conquering Romans built their houses and raised crops in the fertile soil. Elaborate drainage systems were built to dry up the Pontine marshes.

Later, the countryside was taken over by emperors, Popes, and princes for hunting grounds. Drainage was neglected. Little streams could not find their way to the sea, and the water stagnated. Mosquitoes bred unchecked; malaria became a scourge. Gradually the people moved away to more healthful places.

Shepherds grazed their flocks in the deserted lands, playing eerie music on goatskin bagpipes. Bandits lived in caves and lay in wait for travelers on the Roman river and roads. There are no bandits now, but the ghostly music of the shepherds still floats over the rocky hills.

In 1937 the Pontine Marshes were drained. Five canals were joined to a connecting canal, and the swamps dried up. Eucalyptus trees now droop silvery gray leaves between umbrella pines and dark cypresses. Red farmhouses still bear the coats of arms of former noble landlords. In the rich fields, tractors work side by side with teams of white cattle. New towns were built, and people came from overcrowded slums of the big cities to live in them.

The Buried City

More then 2,000 years ago there was a bustling town where the Tiber empties into the Tyrrhenian Sea. This was the city of Ostia (from the Latin word *ostium*, for mouth). It was the chief port of Rome. But the tawny Tiber filled its bed with the silt washed down from the hills, and then the muddy river spilled out into the town.

Emperors and engineers tried to keep the river open for ships and save the city from burial in mud. They dug a new channel for the Tiber southwest of Ostia, making a second river where the port city of Fiumicino now stands. But the silt kept coming.

Modern engineers estimate that the Tiber brings down 300 cubic yards of silt every second. Suppose the silt could be used to build a tower of dirt, 100 feet square at the base. How tall would the tower be at the end of a single day? It would rise thirteen miles.

The silt gradually spread over Ostia and pushed out into the sea. The old town was abandoned. Wind-blown sand buried the city, and memories of it faded away. The shore line moved about two miles out into the sea from Roman times to the present. It is still advancing about twelve feet a year.

Early in the twentieth century, archaeologists began to dig away the sand and silt that covered Ostia. Now half of the old city can be seen. Visitors walk along the narrow cobbled streets that were old before Christ was born.

Decorated walls of temples, houses, baths, the forum, and the theater are still standing. Merchants came from all over the empire to do business in Ostia. They had offices in a square where they chartered ships and made bargains over corn, fruit, fabrics, and the thousands of goods needed by the Romans. Their trademarks are still to be seen

E. Richter

Olive oil was stored hundreds of years ago in these jars at Ostia.

on the mosaic floors in front of the offices. One shows a set of scales. Others have ships and fish and even an elephant. War elephants were brought from Africa and were used as a modern army uses its tanks.

Between the trees, in enclosed plots, earthenware jars are sunk in the ground. Each is big enough to hold over 100 gallons. All kinds of food were packed and stored in these jars, called *amphorae*. In Rome a hill has been formed from broken amphorae. It was once the city rubbish dump.

The walls around the public fountains are worn smooth by generations of leaning arms drawing jars of water. The wine shops have marble counters, shelves, and benches. There are paintings of flowers and fruit on the walls.

Wandering along, you can picture the town as it was in its prosperous days. Bejeweled Asians, bearded Arabs, and swarthy sailors would stand aside as a Roman merchant was carried on a litter into the square. Nubian slaves fanned him with peacock feathers as his Greek slaves wrote down details of the business. The bellowing and bleating of animals mingled with the shouts of seamen and a babble of voices arguing, singing, crying out in pain, or begging for alms.

Fires were dreaded. Naked flaring torches could turn this town of wooden ships, corn, oil and cotton stores into a gigantic bonfire in seconds. Ostia had big barracks for the firemen, who were most important citizens.

Now Ostia dreams in the sun. Students and visitors roam around, lizards sleep on the walls, and laughing boys and girls climb the steps of the theater and look down at the stage where actors played their parts so long ago.

Paul M. Pretsch, Black Star
Part of the ancient city of Ostia, once buried by the Tiber's silt.

Kevin I. Nowlan

Gay umbrellas shade the stalls of hucksters at the Fiumicino dock.

A swing bridge spans the second arm of the Tiber at Fiumicino. Once a fishing village, this town, too, was badly damaged by bombs in World War II. It is a strange mixture of old and new. Streamlined concrete buildings stare blankly down on the harbor where the traditional fishing boats unload their catch. Housewives come with baskets to bargain with the salesmen who shade their stalls with colored umbrellas. Fishermen sit cross-legged on the pier, mending nets that dry in the

Fishing boats at Fiumicino, with modern apartments in background.

sun. A bus fills with passengers going to the Leonardo da Vinci Airport close by. A huge bronze statue of this famous man stands sentinel at one of the newest and finest European airports.

Leonardo da Vinci, the fifteenth century artist, poet, engineer, scientist, and philosopher, was one of the most remarkable and inquisitive men ever born. He studied the laws of gravity, currents of wind and water, human anatomy, the flight of birds, the growth of plants, and the formation of rocks. He asked himself, and everyone else, questions about everything and made notes and sketches of what he learned. He was a skilled artist who drew designs for battle chariots as well as delicate flower studies. He painted the portrait of a woman with a strange smile. She is the Mona Lisa, who has enchanted and puzzled men for 400 years. Leonardo was left-handed, and he wrote in fine small script, usually from right to left of the page. How is this genius connected with a modern airport?

He believed that it was possible for a man to fly in the sky, and he invented a flying machine. He constructed at least one, and in a notebook he wrote, "Tomorrow on the second day of January 1496 I will make the attempt." Another note reads, "I find that if this instrument made with a screw be well made, that is to say, made of linen of which the pores are stopped up with starch, and it be turned swiftly, the said screw will make it spiral in the air and it will rise high." But he warns, "This machine should be tried over a lake and you should carry a long wine skin as a girdle

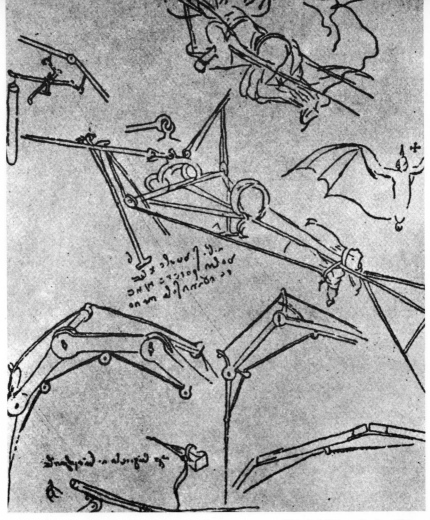

Historical Pictures Service—Chicago

Some of the sketches made by Leonardo da Vinci for a flying machine.

so that in case you fall in you will not be drowned."

Secretly, Leonardo went to the bare Swan Mountain near Fiesole for the test of his flying machine. No one knows what happened, but there is a legend that a huge bird once rose from the mountain and vanished. Leonardo wrote no more about flight, but today his countrymen honor the man whose vision of flying came true.

Dark specks appear on the horizon at Fiumicino. Homecoming fishing boats form into line as though in salute to the towering statue of Leonardo. Transcontinental jet planes drown the cries of wheeling seagulls. Women and children stand waiting for their menfolk—as their ancestors watched for the spreading sails and the flashing oars of the Roman galleys returning to the arms of Father Tiber, the Roman river.

Fishermen make use of a recently built Tiber bridge, Ponte Nuova.

Kevin I. Nowlan

Index